This Reading Journal belongs to:

• • • • • • • • • • • • • • • •

Reading Journal for Children
A book review starter for kids
A reading log for kids & their grown ups

April 2021 Edition

@adaytoremember_journals
adaytoremember.journals@gmail.com

INDEX

4	INTRODUCTION
5	OUR THANK YOU NOTE TO YOU
6	HOW TO USE THIS JOURNAL
7-9	HOW TO GET THE MOST OF READING TIME
10	MY BOOKS REVIEWS

11-13	BOOK 1: _____ DATE: _____
14-16	BOOK 2: _____ DATE: _____
17-19	BOOK 3: _____ DATE: _____
20-22	BOOK 4: _____ DATE: _____
23-25	BOOK 5: _____ DATE: _____
26-28	BOOK 6: _____ DATE: _____
29-31	BOOK 7: _____ DATE: _____
32-34	BOOK 8: _____ DATE: _____
35-37	BOOK 9: _____ DATE: _____
38-40	BOOK 10: _____ DATE: _____
41-43	BOOK 11: _____ DATE: _____
44-46	BOOK 12: _____ DATE: _____
47-49	BOOK 13: _____ DATE: _____
50-52	BOOK 14: _____ DATE: _____
53-55	BOOK 15: _____ DATE: _____

56-58 BOOK 16: _____
DATE: _____

59-61 BOOK 17: _____
DATE: _____

62-64 BOOK 18: _____
DATE: _____

65-67 BOOK 19: _____
DATE: _____

68-70 BOOK 20: _____
DATE: _____

71-73 BOOK 21: _____
DATE: _____

74-76 BOOK 22: _____
DATE: _____

77-79 BOOK 23: _____
DATE: _____

80-82 BOOK 24: _____
DATE: _____

83-85 BOOK 25: _____
DATE: _____

86-88 BOOK 26: _____
DATE: _____

89-91 BOOK 27: _____
DATE: _____

92-94 BOOK 28: _____
DATE: _____

95-97 BOOK 29: _____
DATE: _____

INTRODUCTION

We created this journal thinking about the many benefits and "wonders" that reading can bring to one's life.

Travel to different worlds. Learn good habits. Get exposure to different cultures. Discover the History. Develop empathy and an understanding about feelings.

Become comfortable (and an advocate!) of diversity – of thoughts, of ethnicity, of backgrounds. ..

...there are so many things that reading can do to a child that reinforcing the habit of a young book lover is always a good idea. Or encouraging a kid who needs to read a bit more. And that's exactly what this journal will do!

This reading log will:

- help teachers and caregivers keep track of a child's (assisted) reading,
- and will promote a dialogue between the reader and the child after each reading session,
    - helping kids reflect about what they read and express it,
    - helping them learn how to interpret text, and even improve drawing skills.

This child-friendly book review starter will also help parents, caregivers and children maintain a reading routine.

Kids will look forward to reading & discussion time, and the "big readers" will have a wonderful record of the child's reading progress made over time!

Before you get started we'd like to introduce ourselves and THANK YOU for buying this journal!

We are 2 high school friends just starting a journey of entrepreneurship.
(We're now "grown ups", moms; Carla is based in the USA, and Milena in Brazil).

We are challenging ourselves to create 52 journals this year, 1 per week!
We are so grateful for your support so far, and we invite you to follow our journey.

Your REVIEW means a lot to us!

We hope and believe that this journal will help your kids to look forward their daily reading & discussion time, and the "big readers" will have a wonderful record of the child's assisted reading journey.

And after you try this journal, would you please give us a couple minutes of your time and write a review on Amazon?

As we write this, this journal is brand new and has approximately only 3 reviews on Amazon, so each new one makes a BIG difference.

Your honest review is a big encouragement for us, new creators and sellers, to keep going. And it helps other people find our product, too!

(To leave a review go to the product page on Amazon, scroll down and select "Write a customer review")

Let's be friends! - CONNECT and SHARE with us

We would be thrilled to hear (read) about your journal ideas, or other comments & suggestions you may have. And if you would like to be part of our "launch team", to receive free samples of future journal concepts, please let us know, too!

Instagram: @adaytoremember_journals
Amazon: follow "A Day to Remember Journals"
or email us at: adaytoremember.journals@gmail.com.

And please "tag us" on Instagram when you post about your experiences!
WE WOULD ♡ TO BE PART OF OUR JOURNEY
the same way we feel that you are a BIG part of ours!

xoxo, Carla and Milena

HOW TO USE THIS JOURNAL

Every time you and your child finish reading a story together, fill out a journal entry with information such as:

- Book name, author name;
- Date when it was read;
- Who was the reader;
- What the child thought about the story (ie. was it funny, scary, exciting?);
- Who are the main characters, and where does the story take place;
- What happened in the story;
- What was the child's favorite part and least favorite part of the story;
- How much the child liked the book;
- And a drawing about the story.

You may complete every section or start asking the child just a few questions, and gradually add more as he or she shows enthusiasm to answer more questions. And, of course, you may read the same book(s) several times, as is the case in most homes after kids develop their "favorites".

This is going to be fun... Let's get started!

HOW TO GET THE MOST OF THE READING TIME WITH KIDS

Before Reading Time

Encourage reading pleasure

The moment of reading is supposed to be pleasant and enriching, so try to create a comfortable environment for you and your child.

Avoid creating restrictive "rules" such as assigning a designated space for him/her to read. Your child should see reading as a rest and fun, and we hope that he or she will be comfortable with books anywhere!

Take advantage of this moment to strengthen bonds and have fun with your little one!

Do not remove or stop activities that the child likes to insert the reading

You shouldn't say things such as "turn off the TV and go read a book".

This could make the child perceive reading as a punishment, and could create aversion or resistance to reading, since the book becomes an obstacle to what he/she likes to do (eg. watch TV).

Be patient

The child will not always be excited about the first reading experiences. You may need to sit together many times until you create the habit and insert the reading time into your child's daily routine.

When/if he/she resists, you can try to sit next to the child and leaf through a book, without saying anything. Kids are interested in what their caregivers do and often will want to jump in to participate in the discoveries.

Be the example and don't give up

Read, spread your books around the house, talk enthusiastically about what you are reading at meals or at other times with family.

This will create curiosity for your child and encourage him/her to get immersed in the world of literature.

During Reading Time

Read the exact words of the text to expand your child's vocabulary

When telling the story, read the way the text is written, without taking out seemingly difficult words. This will gradually expand their vocabulary.

If the child asks, explain the meaning of new words using simple examples and synonyms.

Make reading time an adventure

Get into the story with your child and have fun. Imitate sounds of animals and nature.

Make reading a great adventure!

Ask questions and value your child's answers

Ask questions to encourage an understanding of the story. As you read, listen and carefully note the child's comments as they reveal their level of understanding and what they're feeling.

Encourage the child to tell the story in their own way, to make "predictions" (eg. what do you think will happen next?) and celebrate their engagement.

Use books as conversation starters to talk about feelings

Talk about the feelings of the characters and ask if the child has felt the same way.

Take advantage of the themes of the books to have conversations about emotions, behaviors and everyday situations.

For slightly older children

Encourage the child to read the book aloud, and help out where he or she has difficulty. But be careful not to put too much pressure on the child to the point that he or she would feel discouraged from reading; we want the child to feel that this is a moment of leisure at home!

One tip is to start by asking the kid for "help" with reading certain (easy) sentences as you read through a book; or for older kids, asking them to read alternating pages (eg. the kid reads a page, the caregiver reads the next one, so you both read the book together).

You'll make progress step by step. We're excited about this journey!

MY BOOKS REVIEWS

Date:

BOOK:

AUTHOR:

Who read with me:

This book is: (Eg. Fun, Scary, Happy, Sad, Exciting...)

Who is/are the main characters?

Where does the story take place?

In the story, they did a lot of things, such as...
(For older kids: What happened at the beginning, in the middle and at the end?)

What is your favorite part of the book?

Was there a part that you didn't like? (If so, What?)

Did you learn any new words/things with this book?

What would you do if you were in the story?

How much did you like this Book:

Draw or write something about the book

Date:

BOOK:

AUTHOR:

Who read with me:

This book is: (Eg. Fun, Scary, Happy, Sad, Exciting...)

Who is/are the main characters?

Where does the story take place?

In the story, they did a lot of things, such as...
(For older kids: What happened at the beginning, in the middle and at the end?)

What is your favorite part of the book?

Was there a part that you didn't like? (If so, What?)

Did you learn any new words/things with this book?

What would you do if you were in the story?

How much did you like this Book:

Draw or write something about the book

Date:

BOOK:

AUTHOR:

Who read with me:

This book is: (Eg. Fun, Scary, Happy, Sad, Exciting...)

Who is/are the main characters?

Where does the story take place?

In the story, they did a lot of things, such as...
(For older kids: What happened at the beginning, in the middle and at the end?)

What is your favorite part of the book?

Was there a part that you didn't like? (If so, what?)

Did you learn any new words/things with this book?

What would you do if you were in the story?

How much did you like this Book:

Draw or write something about the book

Date:

BOOK:

AUTHOR:

Who read with me:

This book is: (Eg. Fun, Scary, Happy, Sad, Exciting...)

Who is/are the main characters?

Where does the story take place?

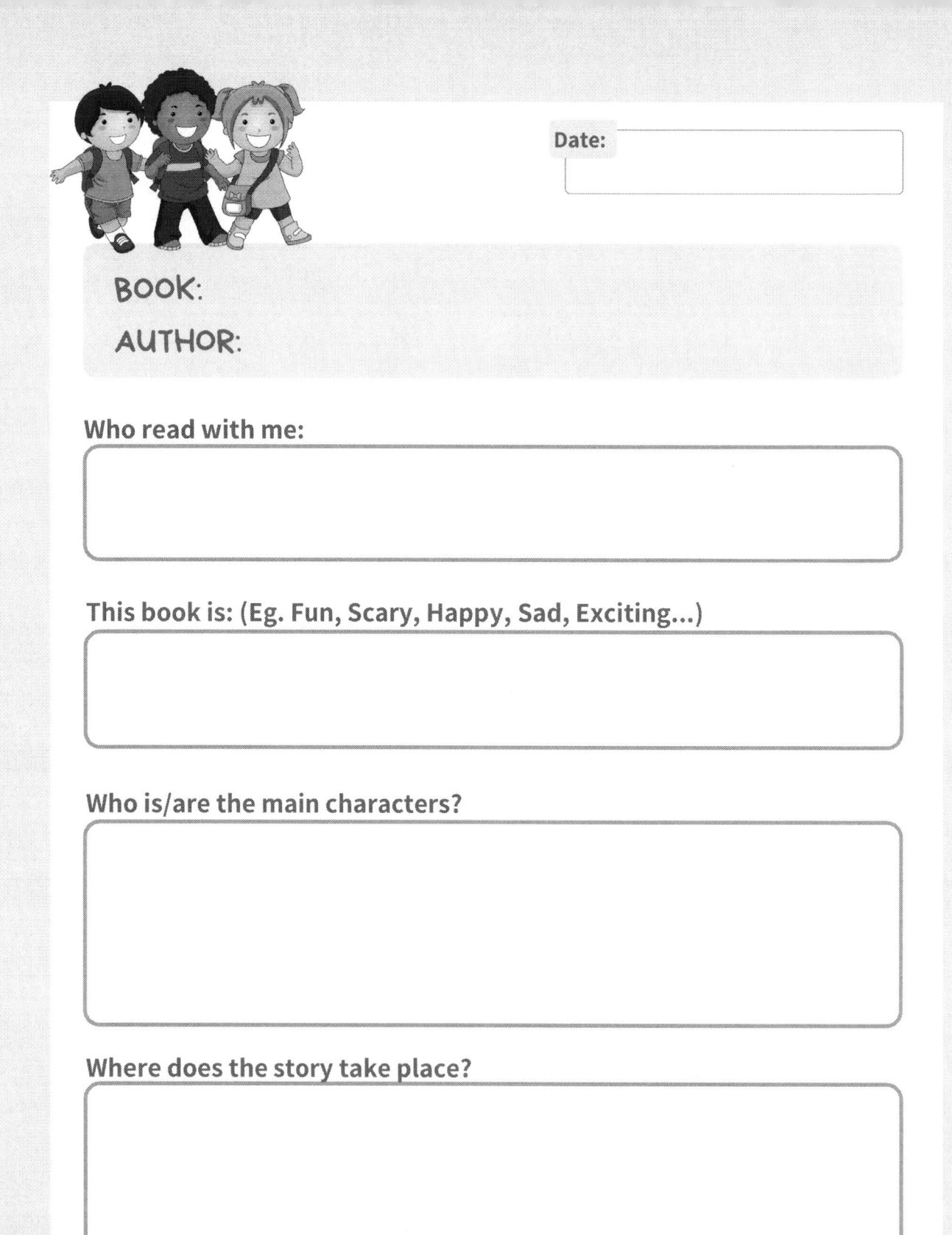

In the story, they did a lot of things, such as...
(For older kids: What happened at the beginning, in the middle and at the end?)

What is your favorite part of the book?

Was there a part that you didn't like? (If so, What?)

Did you learn any new words/things with this book?

What would you do if you were in the story?

How much did you like this Book:

Draw or write something about the book

Date:

BOOK:

AUTHOR:

Who read with me:

This book is: (Eg. Fun, Scary, Happy, Sad, Exciting...)

Who is/are the main characters?

Where does the story take place?

In the story, they did a lot of things, such as...
(For older kids: What happened at the beginning, in the middle and at the end?)

What is your favorite part of the book?

Was there a part that you didn't like? (If so, What?)

Did you learn any new words/things with this book?

What would you do if you were in the story?

How much did you like this Book:

Draw or write something about the book

Date:

BOOK:

AUTHOR:

Who read with me:

This book is: (Eg. Fun, Scary, Happy, Sad, Exciting...)

Who is/are the main characters?

Where does the story take place?

In the story, they did a lot of things, such as...
(For older kids: What happened at the beginning, in the middle and at the end?)

What is your favorite part of the book?

Was there a part that you didn't like? (If so, What?)

Did you learn any new words/things with this book?

What would you do if you were in the story?

How much did you like this Book:

Draw or write something about the book

Date:

BOOK:

AUTHOR:

Who read with me:

This book is: (Eg. Fun, Scary, Happy, Sad, Exciting...)

Who is/are the main characters?

Where does the story take place?

In the story, they did a lot of things, such as...
(For older kids: What happened at the beginning, in the middle and at the end?)

What is your favorite part of the book?

Was there a part that you didn't like? (If so, what?)

Did you learn any new words/things with this book?

What would you do if you were in the story?

How much did you like this Book:

Draw or write something about the book

Date:

BOOK:

AUTHOR:

Who read with me:

This book is: (Eg. Fun, Scary, Happy, Sad, Exciting...)

Who is/are the main characters?

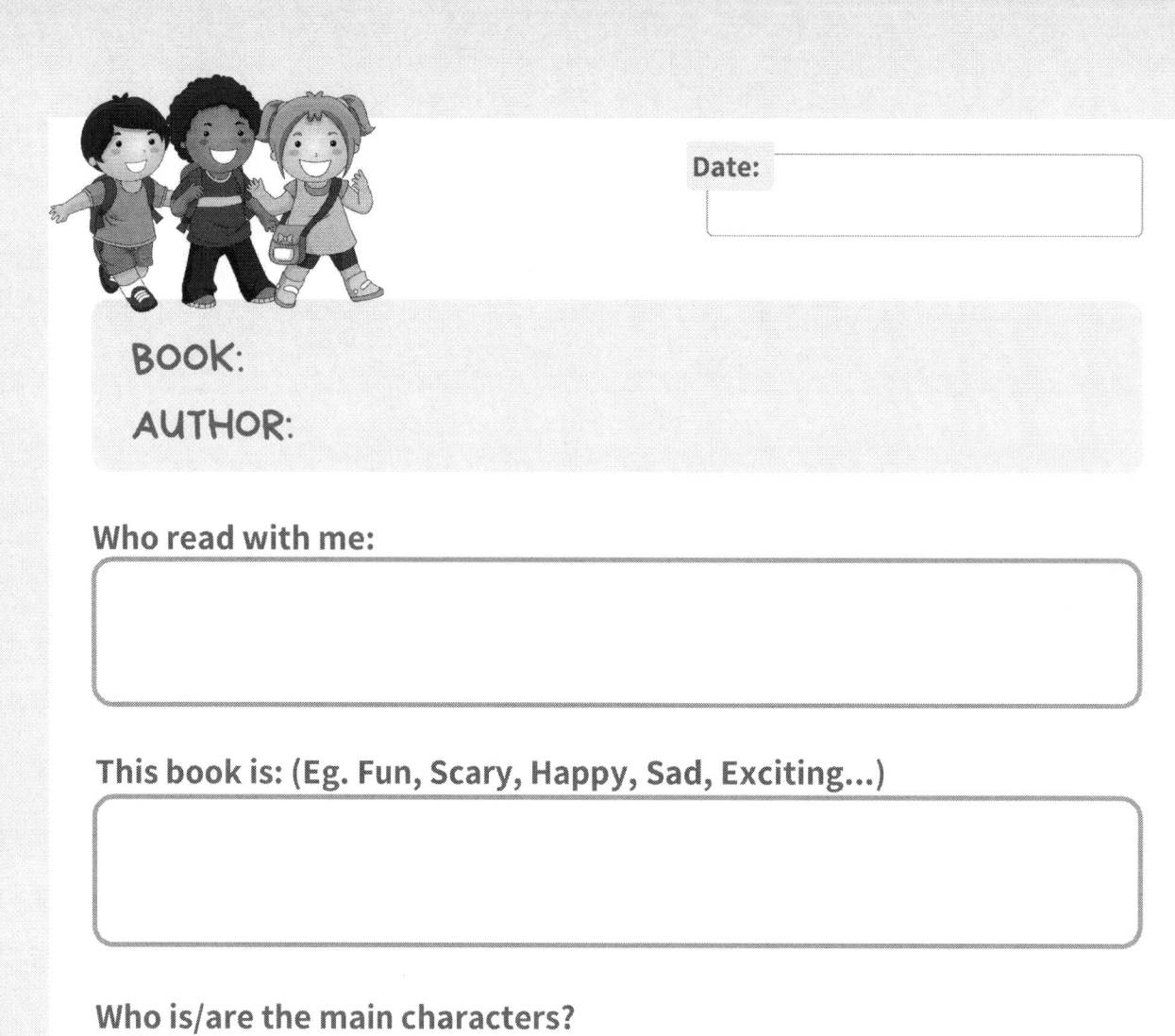

Where does the story take place?

In the story, they did a lot of things, such as...
(For older kids: What happened at the beginning, in the middle and at the end?)

What is your favorite part of the book?

Was there a part that you didn't like? (If so, What?)

Did you learn any new words/things with this book?

What would you do if you were in the story?

How much did you like this Book:

Draw or write something about the book

Date:

BOOK:

AUTHOR:

Who read with me:

This book is: (Eg. Fun, Scary, Happy, Sad, Exciting...)

Who is/are the main characters?

Where does the story take place?

In the story, they did a lot of things, such as...
(For older kids: What happened at the beginning, in the middle and at the end?)

What is your favorite part of the book?

Was there a part that you didn't like? (If so, What?)

Did you learn any new words/things with this book?

What would you do if you were in the story?

How much did you like this Book:

Draw or write something about the book

Date:

BOOK:

AUTHOR:

Who read with me:

This book is: (Eg. Fun, Scary, Happy, Sad, Exciting...)

Who is/are the main characters?

Where does the story take place?

In the story, they did a lot of things, such as...
(For older kids: What happened at the beginning, in the middle and at the end?)

What is your favorite part of the book?

Was there a part that you didn't like? (If so, What?)

Did you learn any new words/things with this book?

What would you do if you were in the story?

How much did you like this Book:

Draw or write something about the book

Date:

BOOK:

AUTHOR:

Who read with me:

This book is: (Eg. Fun, Scary, Happy, Sad, Exciting...)

Who is/are the main characters?

Where does the story take place?

In the story, they did a lot of things, such as...
(For older kids: What happened at the beginning, in the middle and at the end?)

What is your favorite part of the book?

Was there a part that you didn't like? (If so, what?)

Did you learn any new words/things with this book?

What would you do if you were in the story?

How much did you like this Book:

Draw or write something about the book

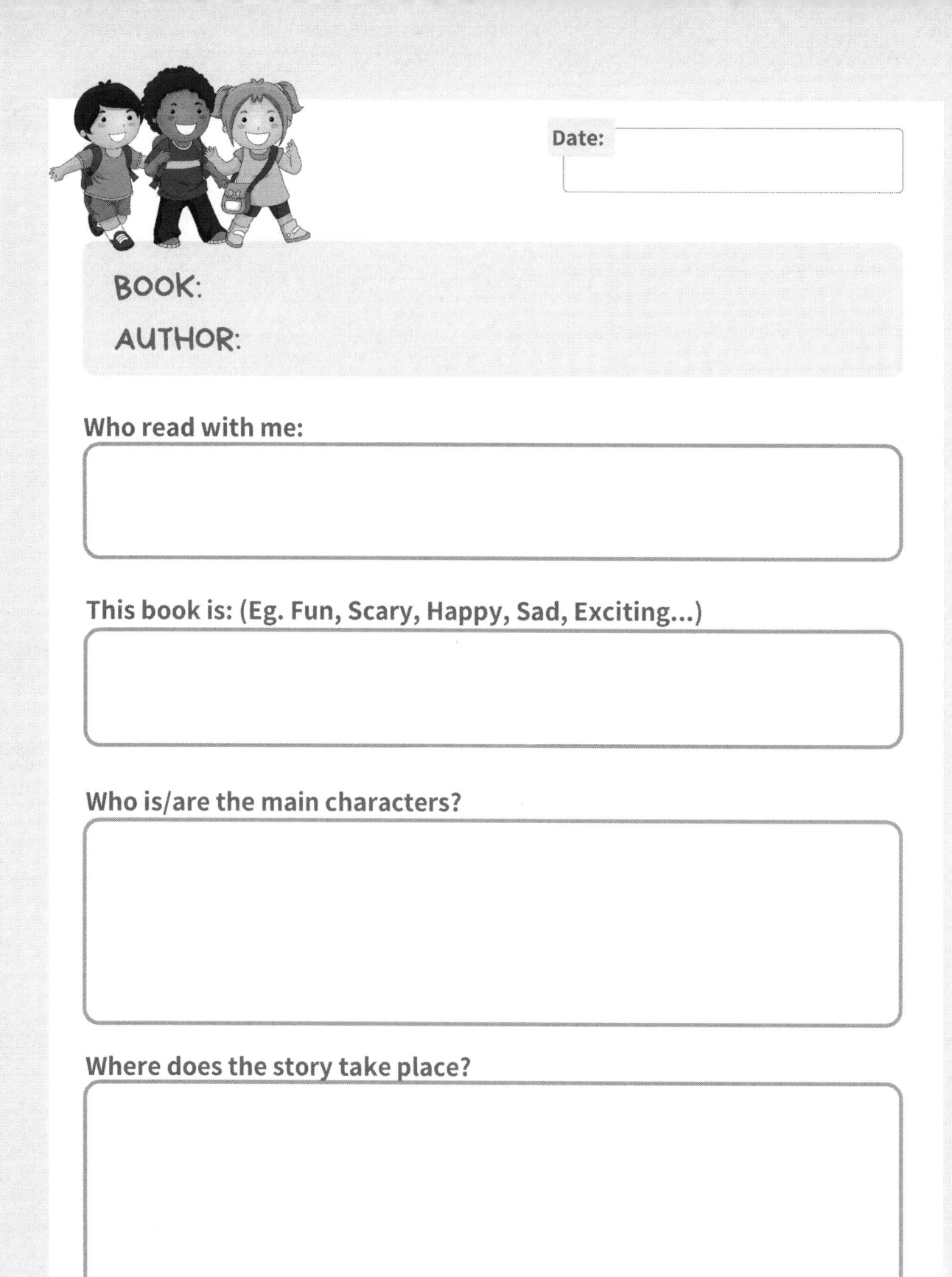

Date:

BOOK:

AUTHOR:

Who read with me:

This book is: (Eg. Fun, Scary, Happy, Sad, Exciting…)

Who is/are the main characters?

Where does the story take place?

In the story, they did a lot of things, such as...
(For older kids: What happened at the beginning, in the middle and at the end?)

What is your favorite part of the book?

Was there a part that you didn't like? (If so, What?)

Did you learn any new words/things with this book?

What would you do if you were in the story?

How much did you like this Book:

Draw or write something about the book

Date:

BOOK:

AUTHOR:

Who read with me:

This book is: (Eg. Fun, Scary, Happy, Sad, Exciting…)

Who is/are the main characters?

Where does the story take place?

In the story, they did a lot of things, such as...
(For older kids: What happened at the beginning, in the middle and at the end?)

What is your favorite part of the book?

Was there a part that you didn't like? (If so, What?)

Did you learn any new words/things with this book?

What would you do if you were in the story?

How much did you like this Book:

Draw or write something about the book

Date:

BOOK:

AUTHOR:

Who read with me:

This book is: (Eg. Fun, Scary, Happy, Sad, Exciting...)

Who is/are the main characters?

Where does the story take place?

In the story, they did a lot of things, such as...
(For older kids: What happened at the beginning, in the middle and at the end?)

What is your favorite part of the book?

Was there a part that you didn't like? (If so, What?)

Did you learn any new words/things with this book?

What would you do if you were in the story?

How much did you like this Book:

Draw or write something about the book

Date:

BOOK:

AUTHOR:

Who read with me:

This book is: (Eg. Fun, Scary, Happy, Sad, Exciting…)

Who is/are the main characters?

Where does the story take place?

In the story, they did a lot of things, such as...
(For older kids: What happened at the beginning, in the middle and at the end?)

What is your favorite part of the book?

Was there a part that you didn't like? (If so, what?)

Did you learn any new words/things with this book?

What would you do if you were in the story?

How much did you like this Book:

Draw or write something about the book

Date:

BOOK:

AUTHOR:

Who read with me:

This book is: (Eg. Fun, Scary, Happy, Sad, Exciting...)

Who is/are the main characters?

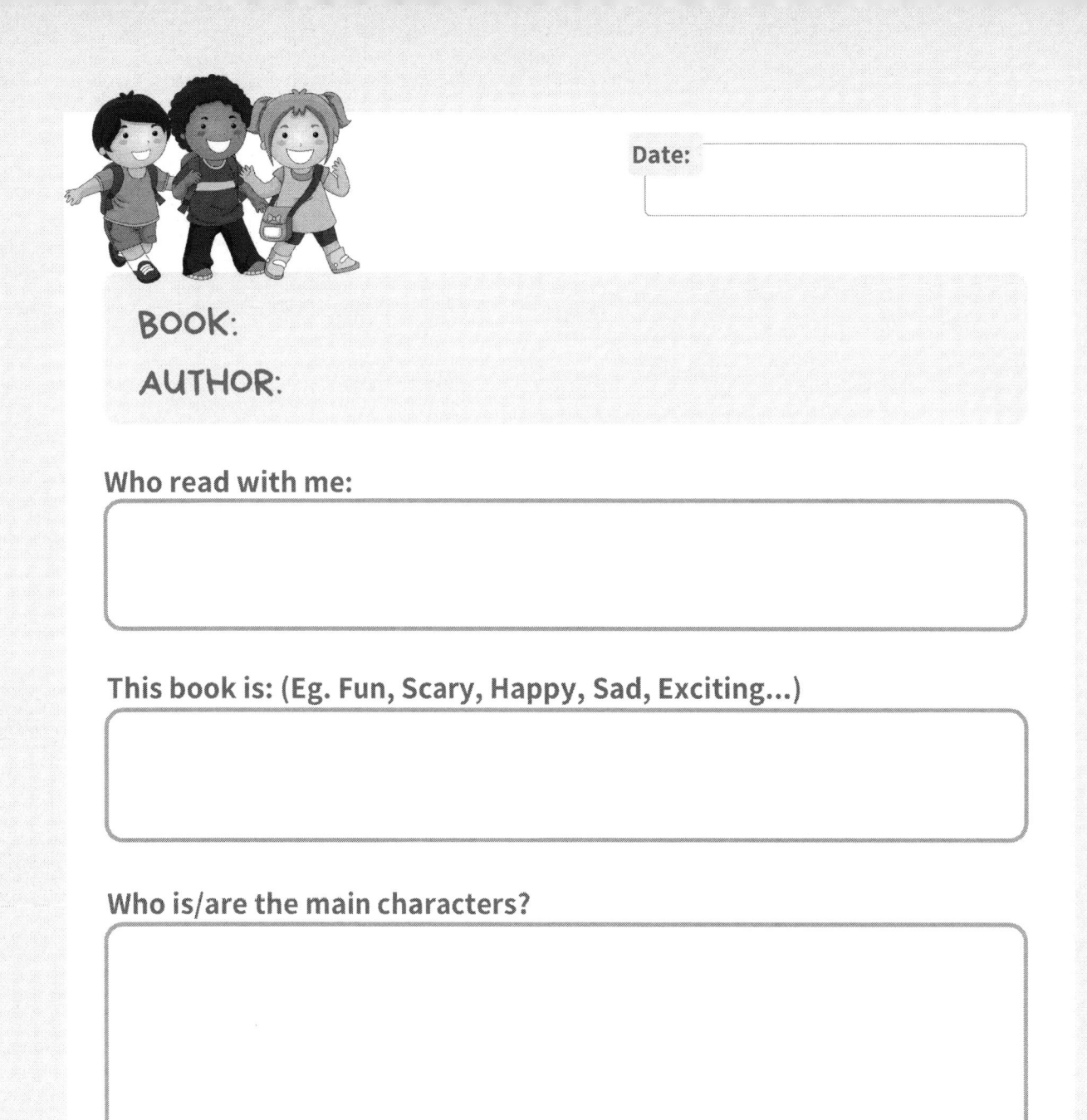

Where does the story take place?

In the story, they did a lot of things, such as...
(For older kids: What happened at the beginning, in the middle and at the end?)

What is your favorite part of the book?

Was there a part that you didn't like? (If so, What?)

Did you learn any new words/things with this book?

What would you do if you were in the story?

How much did you like this Book:

Draw or write something about the book

Date:

BOOK:

AUTHOR:

Who read with me:

This book is: (Eg. Fun, Scary, Happy, Sad, Exciting...)

Who is/are the main characters?

Where does the story take place?

In the story, they did a lot of things, such as...
(For older kids: What happened at the beginning, in the middle and at the end?)

What is your favorite part of the book?

Was there a part that you didn't like? (If so, What?)

Did you learn any new words/things with this book?

What would you do if you were in the story?

How much did you like this Book:

Draw or write something about the book

Date:

BOOK:

AUTHOR:

Who read with me:

This book is: (Eg. Fun, Scary, Happy, Sad, Exciting...)

Who is/are the main characters?

Where does the story take place?

In the story, they did a lot of things, such as…
(For older kids: What happened at the beginning, in the middle and at the end?)

What is your favorite part of the book?

Was there a part that you didn't like? (If so, What?)

Did you learn any new words/things with this book?

What would you do if you were in the story?

How much did you like this Book:

Draw or write something about the book

Date:

BOOK:

AUTHOR:

Who read with me:

This book is: (Eg. Fun, Scary, Happy, Sad, Exciting...)

Who is/are the main characters?

Where does the story take place?

In the story, they did a lot of things, such as...
(For older kids: What happened at the beginning, in the middle and at the end?)

What is your favorite part of the book?

Was there a part that you didn't like? (If so, what?)

Did you learn any new words/things with this book?

What would you do if you were in the story?

How much did you like this Book:

Draw or write something about the book

Date:

BOOK:

AUTHOR:

Who read with me:

This book is: (Eg. Fun, Scary, Happy, Sad, Exciting...)

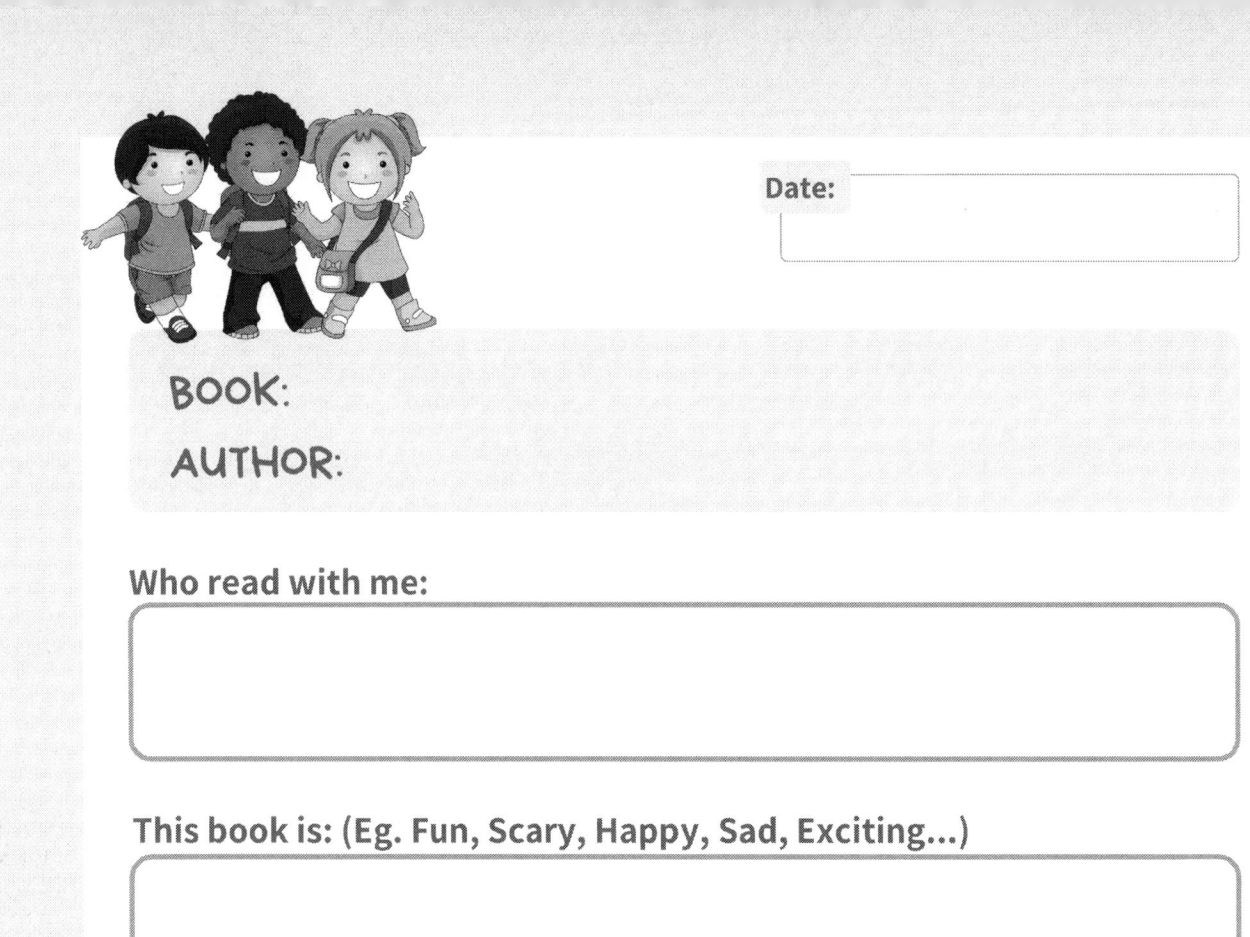

Who is/are the main characters?

Where does the story take place?

In the story, they did a lot of things, such as...
(For older kids: What happened at the beginning, in the middle and at the end?)

What is your favorite part of the book?

Was there a part that you didn't like? (If so, What?)

Did you learn any new words/things with this book?

What would you do if you were in the story?

How much did you like this Book:

Draw or write something about the book

Date:

BOOK:

AUTHOR:

Who read with me:

This book is: (Eg. Fun, Scary, Happy, Sad, Exciting...)

Who is/are the main characters?

Where does the story take place?

In the story, they did a lot of things, such as...
(For older kids: What happened at the beginning, in the middle and at the end?)

What is your favorite part of the book?

Was there a part that you didn't like? (If so, What?)

Did you learn any new words/things with this book?

What would you do if you were in the story?

How much did you like this Book:

Draw or write something about the book

Date:

BOOK:

AUTHOR:

Who read with me:

This book is: (Eg. Fun, Scary, Happy, Sad, Exciting...)

Who is/are the main characters?

Where does the story take place?

In the story, they did a lot of things, such as...
(For older kids: What happened at the beginning, in the middle and at the end?)

What is your favorite part of the book?

Was there a part that you didn't like? (If so, What?)

Did you learn any new words/things with this book?

What would you do if you were in the story?

How much did you like this Book:

Draw or write something about the book

Date:

BOOK:

AUTHOR:

Who read with me:

This book is: (Eg. Fun, Scary, Happy, Sad, Exciting...)

Who is/are the main characters?

Where does the story take place?

In the story, they did a lot of things, such as...
(For older kids: What happened at the beginning, in the middle and at the end?)

What is your favorite part of the book?

Was there a part that you didn't like? (If so, what?)

Did you learn any new words/things with this book?

What would you do if you were in the story?

How much did you like this Book:

Draw or write something about the book

Date:

BOOK:

AUTHOR:

Who read with me:

This book is: (Eg. Fun, Scary, Happy, Sad, Exciting...)

Who is/are the main characters?

Where does the story take place?

In the story, they did a lot of things, such as…
(For older kids: What happened at the beginning, in the middle and at the end?)

What is your favorite part of the book?

Was there a part that you didn't like? (If so, What?)

Did you learn any new words/things with this book?

What would you do if you were in the story?

How much did you like this Book:

Draw or write something about the book

Date:

BOOK:

AUTHOR:

Who read with me:

This book is: (Eg. Fun, Scary, Happy, Sad, Exciting…)

Who is/are the main characters?

Where does the story take place?

In the story, they did a lot of things, such as...
(For older kids: What happened at the beginning, in the middle and at the end?)

What is your favorite part of the book?

Was there a part that you didn't like? (If so, What?)

Did you learn any new words/things with this book?

What would you do if you were in the story?

How much did you like this Book:

Draw or write something about the book

Date:

BOOK:

AUTHOR:

Who read with me:

This book is: (Eg. Fun, Scary, Happy, Sad, Exciting…)

Who is/are the main characters?

Where does the story take place?

In the story, they did a lot of things, such as...
(For older kids: What happened at the beginning, in the middle and at the end?)

What is your favorite part of the book?

Was there a part that you didn't like? (If so, What?)

Did you learn any new words/things with this book?

What would you do if you were in the story?

How much did you like this Book:

Draw or write something about the book

Date:

BOOK:

AUTHOR:

Who read with me:

This book is: (Eg. Fun, Scary, Happy, Sad, Exciting...)

Who is/are the main characters?

Where does the story take place?

In the story, they did a lot of things, such as...
(For older kids: What happened at the beginning, in the middle and at the end?)

What is your favorite part of the book?

Was there a part that you didn't like? (If so, what?)

Did you learn any new words/things with this book?

What would you do if you were in the story?

How much did you like this Book: 🙂 😐 ☹️

Draw or write something about the book

Thank you For Using This Journal. We Hope you liked it!

We are on a journey of publishing 52 journals this year!
We would love to invite you to check out one of our other Journals:

Kids

READING JOURNAL FOR CHILDREN:
This journal was created to encourage kids to have reading & discussion time with their grown ups. It also includes key recommendations for the grown ups on how to make the most of reading time with kids. And the "big readers" will have a wonderful record of the child's assisted reading journey.

NATURE OBSERVATION JOURNAL FOR CHILDREN:
This "draw and write journal" will encourage you to spend family time in contact with nature, even if you live in a city.
With it you will record your child's nature observations and will encourage him/her to draw what he/she saw, or represent how he/she felt while in contact with nature

KIDS ACTIVITIES JOURNAL FOR CHILDREN:
This journal was designed with the goal to support families in developing a healthier, more organized and efficient routine of activities while raising their children. It will help you plan for playful activities, games & hobbies with children, in addition to encouraging them to do school work and help with chores.

Happiness, Stress release & Reconnection

HAPPINESS FROM THE SOUL:
This "self-therapy" happiness journal is exactly what you need to start to implement daily 3 things that a Harvard professor teaches: Organize your errands / Message someone important/ Write a journal entry. After a few days doing this, you're very likely to start feeling happier!

Therapy Journals

THERAPY JOURNAL:
This is a journal with prompts (questions and suggestions), and it was designed to support you during 30 therapy sessions, no matter how often they take place (ie. it will be ok if you use it twice a week, once a week, or once every 2 weeks). It also includes important recommendations that will help you make the most of your therapy sessions.

VIRTUAL THERAPY JOURNAL:
Similar to the above, this is a journal with prompts (questions and suggestions), and it was designed to support you during 30 virtual therapy sessions, no matter how often they take place (eg. twice a week, once a week, or once every 2 weeks).
The difference it that this journal gives recommendations for VIRTUAL sessions.

THERAPY SESSIONS JOURNAL:
If you like to write in LINED journals, this is the one for you! This journal also has prompts (questions & suggestions), and it was designed to support you during 6 months of therapy (with weekly therapy sessions, ie. 4-5 sessions per month). This therapy journal will help you make the most of your therapy and self-reflection sessions.!

COUPLES THERAPY JOURNAL:
This journal has 3 main spaces for you to write in: (1) a space for you to write what is the focus of each session, (2) a space to capture how your partner is thinking and feeling and what he/she is sharing, (3) and finally a space for you to write your own insights & takeaways during counseling sessions. The right choice for people attending Couples Therapy!

Our journals are available on Amazon in English, German, French and Italian
(with more languages to come soon).

Motherhood & Family

THINGS I LOVE (AND NOT SO MUCH) ABOUT BEING A MOM:
This is a blank/lined journal for moms to write about motherhood experiences – good and bad days – and make the most out of all of their days. It will help you normalize what's normal, feel more relaxed and clear your mind. Over time you will have a beautiful collection of "motherhood moments"!

MOMMY & ME A KEEPSAKE JOURNAL
This is a journal with prompts that will guide a mother to write about her memories and prepare her children to thrive in life by sharing important advice and lessons. Fill any page, at any time, until you complete the journal, or fell that "it's ready". Then give it (back) as a treasured gift to your child!

GRANDMA, YOUR STORY IS A GIFT JOURNAL
The best gift for grandma! This journal will prompt a grandmother to write about her memories, special moments with the grandkid, and precious advice. Grandmas will love to share their story, and when "ready" this journal will be a treasured gift to future generations!

AUNTIE LOVES YOU FOREVER JOURNAL
This is a journal with prompts that will guide an auntie to write about her memories and prepare her nephews & nieces to thrive in life by sharing important advice and lessons. Fill any page, at any time, until you complete the journal, or fell that "it's ready". Then give this precious gift (back) to your nephews & nieces!

... and more!

Check our full collection on Amazon.

Join our "Launch Team"

If you would like to to receive free samples of future journals to help us validating concepts, with cover visual selection and more, please let us know!

--> *New journals are launched almost every week!* <--

Connect with us & leave your Review on Amazon

We would love to stay connected, and receive you comments or suggestions.
Follow / message / tag us / leave a review:
- on Amazon: A Day to Remember Journals
- Instagram: @adaytoremember_journals
- OR email: adaytoremember.journals@gmail.com

We'd really appreciate if you could leave an honest review on Amazon (even just the star rating helps us a lot!)

With much gratitude,
Carla and Milena

Made in the USA
Middletown, DE
16 May 2021